What Cana
about Davi~

"David McFadden is such an essential writer for us. His wonderful poems before and after *Gypsy Guitar*, his great *Trip Around the Lakes* series, feel to me the central unofficial voice of our time. He has always kept us close to the earth with his humour and his wandering off the beaten path of literature." **Michael Ondaatje**

"David McFadden's poems come across as passages in a long, thoughtful, roaming conversation about matters no less deeply serious for sometimes being utterly frivolous. As the title of one his books, *There'll Be Another*, suggests, it all seems easy—this stroll from one poem to the next, this leap between stanzas—but that's part of McFadden's art. There won't be another like him. Let's treasure the one we've got; the conversation of his poems includes us." **Stephanie Bolster**

"Dave McFadden's attention to writing has always been top-notch, right from when he published *Mountain* magazine in the early '60s through many years of a wide range of poetry, prose, teaching, editing, and just being open to the beauty of language. In my generation he's a master." **Fred Wah**

"His words would rip a hole in the night." **Lillian Necakov**

"David McFadden has won every book prize ever lodged in a secret corner of everyone's heart, his acceptance speech echoing in our heads." **George Bowering**

"Part rascal, part rogue, David McFadden is one of Canada's chief mischief makers. He condenses essential wisdom and offers it generously. I'm made more human by reading his work." **Sandra Ridley**

"The world is full of wonders, but this can be easily forgotten. The poetry of David W. McFadden is a manual for restoring that sense of wonder. I'm quite certain reading it has improved my life tremendously." **Paul Vermeersch**

"David McFadden is one of the purest and most radiant poetic souls of our time." **Steve Venright**

"DM's work creates, plumbs, makes nervous, the stillness at the centre of being, and the loudness at the edge of picnics. It is involved with existence. Affects, and alters it." **Beverley Daurio**

"My introduction to the work of David McFadden was when I discovered his great book *Poems Worth Knowing* back in the '70s. It was on the same poetry shelf with Bukowski, Brautigan, Kerouac and others, in a small independent bookstore. The glassine slip and pink cover killed me. I've loved his work ever since." **Michael Dennis**

"I first came across David McFadden's poetry in the 1970s when I read *A Knight in Dried Plums*. I was immediately drawn to his work. Here were poems that were relaxed and yet so intense that they were scary. I wondered, how does he do this? No answer. Now, years later and after reading many McFadden poems, I say he is unique and I call it pure poetry." **Heather Cadsby**

"I loved the breathtaking story of following the cow who spent all night swimming across one of the Great Lakes." **Judith Copithorne**

"David McFadden's profound understanding of the human condition and his compassion for his fellow beings are expansively conveyed in the poems in *Why Are You So Sad?* The poems provide space and place for reflection. I revisit these poems often." **Nelson Ball**

"David McFadden's poetry is probably the poetry most often read aloud at my house. I can't remember a time when one of McFadden's books wasn't on my husband's nightstand, and I recall an entire summer where pretty much all we read was *Why Are You So Sad?* We love McFadden's poetry because it is so curious and funny and often surprising and surreal. We also appreciate how often he gets in a dig at George Bowering! But really the thing we love the most is the intimacy McFadden creates between the voices in his poems and his readers. We never feel very far from the experience of the poem and that is why they fit into our lives so very well. His is a broad talent, a unique voice and real vision. There's no one else like him." **Elizabeth Bachinsky**

"For me, the pleasure in David's writing is the wonder, curiosity and humour with which he approaches the big and small alike. His penchant for wordplay and life's little quirks transport us beyond laughter to a poignant place where, indeed, 'Horses love to have their eyes kissed by nuns.'" **Lesley McAllister**

"David McFadden's poetry thrills and dazzles, yet it's so friendly and unpretentious. I don't know how he packs all that wonder, wisdom and thought-provocation into such deceptively plainspoken verse, but the result is alchemical and glorious to read." **Peter Norman**

"I've spent way more time with Dave's poems than with him over the last 40 years. His poems helped raise me as a poet. And for that, I love him, pure and simple." **Jim Smith**

"As I was starting out, David McFadden's work was what gave me permission to proceed by showing me that what I wanted to do was possible. I still look forward to new work from McFadden because it continues to encourage, to inspire, to amaze." **Michael Blouin**

Shouting Your Name

Down the Well

Tankas and Haiku

Also by David W. McFadden

Shouting Your Name
Down the Well

Tankas and Haiku

David W. McFadden

Mansfield Press

Library and Archives Canada Cataloguing in Publication

McFadden, David, 1940-
[Poems. Selections]
      Shouting your name down a well : tankas and haiku / David W.
McFadden.

ISBN 978-1-77126-041-1 (pbk.)

      I. Title.

PS8525.F32.A6 2014   C811'.54   C2014-900978-X

Editor for the press: Stuart Ross
Cover photo & design: Stuart Ross

The publication of *Shouting Your Name Down the Well* has
been generously supported by the Canada Council for the
Arts and the Ontario Arts Council.

Mansfield Press Inc.
25 Mansfield Avenue, Toronto, Ontario, Canada M6J 2A9
Publisher: Denis De Klerck
www.mansfieldpress.net

This book is dedicated to Merlin Homer the Great!
(And I mean it.)

"No man knows the smell
of his own bean-paste."

Basho (1644-1694)

Hard to be serene
When every minute or so
Another frog of
Five or seven syllables
Plops into the sylvan pool.

Why thank you, Merlin—
I am very pleased to know
My haikus please you.

I'll never win a
Prize for my poetry, but
That's okay because
Everyone already knows
I need no encouragement.

Have a lovely walk.
But the wind is ferocious—
Don't get eaten up.

Nice to have you back
And in such good form of course—
I hope you slept well!

Merlin says her cats
Have to do many things, like
Inventory checks.

Don't ride your bike in
Toronto's busy traffic.
If you died I'd die.

Four in the morning—
A solitary gull cries
Out over the sea.
At first I thought it was you
Anguished in the other room.

They were in bed, he
Reading my poems to her.
    She turned to him, said:
"Ohh! I love Genmai." This was
Told to me by him, sadly.

    Last chance to hit balls
For five hundred and twenty
    Miles (sign in *Tin Cup*).

    Long walk. Now I'm home.
Not sure if it helped at all—
    Think I'll have a nap.

    I am so weary
All I can do is drop off—
    You are wide awake.

All my life I took
Size eight and a half in shoes.
　　　Today at Town Shoes
The salesman tells me I'm wrong—
I take nine and a half now.

　　　There are wonderful
People in the world but I'm
　　　Not one, nor my friends.

　　　Do you believe that?
Let's experiment, okay?
　　　We can die sweetly!

　　　It seems as if a
Series of tiny earthquakes
　　　Has hit Vancouver
Since I was last here. All the
Buildings seem a bit askew.

Sam says a comet
Will hit the moon, which will bounce
The Earth into the
Sun like a big snooker game.
Refuses to see a shrink.

Everywhere I look
In snow and rocks, faces of
Aboriginals.

She says I look my
Age. Why would she lie like that?
It's impossible.

Annie heard someone
Sawing wood in the backyard
Long after midnight.
Turned out it was just the cheap
Alarm clock I thought to bring.

Staggered home last night
With many brilliant insights—
All I recall is
The city's the same as the
Country, only more buildings.

Sixteen peaches sit
Ripening slowly on the
Branch of my window.

If I couldn't be
Me I'd like to be either
John Wayne or my mom.

When did you write this?
I hope you can look at my
Face and be happy.

In my dream last night
My girl friend was so tiny
      She could wear dolls' clothes—
All the fellows were trying
To steal her away from me.

Anne just reads novels—
Ian books about the war.
      But once long ago
They read Takuboku's poems
Aloud at a wedding feast.

Since I discovered
Takuboku my fingers
      Are numb with counting.

Ian says that when
I walk down Government Street
      Blossoms fall from trees.

On the ferry with
Lola Lemire Tostevin.
She is just like me—
But she's luckier, she has
A seven-syllable name!

Late at night I sit
Watching the fish in the tank.
Their eyes never close.
They're like little wind-up toys.
Wonder if they know they're real.

Underwear and socks
I'll be wearing when I die—
Have I bought them yet?

A lovely lady—
How odd to see her walking
Such an ugly dog!

Everyone has a
Rough time of it in this life.
A fly in a web
Watching the spider approach—
How is it different from me?

I'm eight years old and
I've read *Peter Pan* eight times.
Now for my ice cream.

I was on one of
Those happy drugs for three months
And liked it okay.
But soon I got nostalgic
For a little misery.

Beside my bedside—
Takuboku's *Poems to Eat*
Placed by dear old friends.

She asks about the
Eyeball in my ring. It's a
Symbol, I say, of
Consciousness, our greatest prize.
"No it's not." She walks away.

A long time ago
I pulled a thorn from out of
My friend Ian's foot.
So now anything I need
He gives it to me freely.

Got a card from George—
He's in Capetown meeting with
Batman, Superman,
And several other guys I
Met in Montevideo!

If he doesn't like
Your opinions, Ian will
      Hand you a small card—
"You are cordially in-
Vited to go fuck yourself."

      In Seattle, it's
Raining heavily and cold—
      Ducks dozing on docks.

      I'm behind the lines
Sending men to certain death.
      Above the muddy
Battlefield is a vision—
A ghostly CN Tower.

      All those bad things that
I remember from the past
      Are really nothing.

Most couples argue
Even about silly things:
        Whether they should stroll
The decks of the ferry boat
Clockwise or counterclockwise.

        Late at night I sit
Laughing at Gary Larson's
        Wiener-dog cartoons.
Everyone else is sleeping.
I wonder what they're dreaming.

        The old cat happens
To be walking across the
        Pitch-dark room as I
Thoughtlessly flick on the light.
He freezes for a moment.

No name-dropping but
I met Yevtushenko once.
　　He told me he thought
We are all equal because
We all have to die someday.

　　Anne thinks I'm sleeping,
Talks about me to Ian.
　　Tells him all about
Taking me to the shoe store
And so on. I don't listen.

　　The mind is an eye.
It has its openings and
　　Closings. When open
It sees only itself, when
Closed it sees nothing at all.

My name is Moby-Dick.
Swimming through the seven seas
Is my life and joy.
I like to come near the shore
And squirt people with my love.

All-knowing God, why
Today of all days do I
Have to have the shits?

Our ancestors wiped
Themselves with leaves. We've progressed.
We do it with trees.

Sunday morning: Anne,
Ian, Sheena and Hailey
Are sad and groggy.
I'm glad I didn't drink much,
Being sad is bad enough.

An evangelist
On Seattle radio
        Begs his listeners
To make out their wills to him.
I would never sink that low!

        Although burnt beyond
Recognition the police
        Were still able to
Identify the victim—
Actual TV report!

        Something I've never
Done before I did today
        Four times and I'm glad.
No one can guess what it was.
And I'm not going to say.

I'm the biggest jerk
In Toronto—my hatred
Is all for myself.

Everlasting God,
Is it possible to waste
Time and if so how?

Nobody must know
Anything about me. Fame
Is a house on fire.

My friends complain I
Ignore them for months and then
I'm all over them.
I think it's something to do
With my lousy work habits.

Here is Issa's snail
Slowly, slowly climbing the
        Old Empress Hotel.

A cat named Siam
Sits on my right thigh although
        More solid resting
Spots could be found. And he looks
In my eyes, reading my mind.

They've just returned from
A long camping trip. "Was it
        In tents?" "Yes, very."

The only money
Worth having comes in the mail
        Unexpectedly.

Somebody wrote on
Lenin's tomb—"An Australian
    Was here." Quite a hop!

It's raining. A small
White poodle looks up to see
    Where it's coming from.

Thirty years ago
I asked Victor Coleman how
    He got from one word
To the other. He tells me
He's still thinking about it.

The life of Genmai—
It's like eating chocolate bars
    Morning, noon and night.

McFadden's funny—
He's like eating peach yogurt
          Morning, noon and night.

          Until I felt your
Essential heat I didn't
          Know how cold I was.

          My heart's lip whispers—
"You're doing great. You're going
          To be famous yet."
But I don't want fame, at least
Not before Victor Coleman.

          I'm pushing for this
Moment not to become too
          Overly poignant.

                    (after Victor Coleman)

Insects make the world
Go round go round go round go
Round go round insects.

Oh, my God! Even
Victor Coleman has an e-
Mail address these days!
Does anyone know what I
Did with my stamp collection?

Annie calls Ian
Mister Important. Ian
Points to a floating
Balloon and declares that the
Ancients would have called it God.

Genmai is happy
As can be. He sleeps all night
And wakes up smiling.

(after Merlin Homer)

Life is an endless
Struggle of hopeless changes
And the odds of time.
P.S. There is LSD
Underneath the postage stamp.

For a limited
Time only. Click here for a
Free trip to your heart.

Too much drink last night.
My hand was in the fire.
I didn't know it.
Today I have a blister
And I'm in a mescal fog.

I'm sorry. Is God
A hypocrite? Or am I
A haiku pervert?

Something I've never
Done before I did today
        Four times and I'm glad.
No one can guess what it was.
Something about poetry.

Anne shows me photos
From years ago showing me
        Wearing for a joke
The kind of glasses that now
I soberly wear each day.

Five yellow tulips
Bend towards the light as if
        They'd never been cut.

How cruel of me! When
Those five yellow tulips have
        Bent I turn the vase.

The five tulips have
Spread their petals and displayed
Five dust-black stamens
And one tripartite yellow
Pistil in the heart of each.

When I see things I
Always want to draw them. I
Forget I can't draw.

She was depressed. I
Was smitten. Now she's better
And I can't stand her.

There's a smokestack on
My television set. How
Strange, how droll, how—oops!
It's not a smokestack, it's an
Empty toilet paper roll.

I sleep so deeply
Sometimes people think I'm dead—
Errors can be made!
Could Robertson Davies have
Written one more trilogy?

What a wonderful
Position to be in. Not
Caring what I write
But only how I write it
And why, where or sometimes when.

My head is full of
Honey. The honey's full of
Twigs and dying bees.
Sometimes I remember things
I haven't thought of for years.

Last thought at night, first
Thought in the morning, but not
Always the same thought.

I call my lyre a
Heavenly tortoise-shell—and
It begins to speak.

(after Sappho)

A little insect
In the silent house made a
Scary creaking sound.

Snow melts and icy
Water overflows the eaves.
This is the house where
Forty-nine summers ago
Hugh Garner wrote *Cabbagetown*.

How rude she was on
The phone last night insisting
On singing two songs
All the way through when she knew
I was desperately tired.

Who has the edge? The
One who forgets or the one
Who is forgotten?

Does it get as bad
For you as it gets for me?
It gets pretty bad.

What's an old guy like
You doing working so late?
Ten blocks of silence—
"Can't think of anything I'd
Rather be doing right now."

Please God don't let me
Die one minute before I've
Spent all my money!

It's April and she's
Moving into a new flat.
She'll be settled by
The time the lilacs and the
Chestnut trees are blossoming.

At three a.m. when
All the traffic disappears—
Electricity!

Kate tells Densher that
Milly's been seeing Luke Strett.
Consumption, perhaps?
The book falls out of my hand
Into Lake Ontario.

Strange thoughts pop into
Emptiness—the liquor store
Near my Grandma's place
Where I'd stop to pick up a
Bottle of Scotch for her health.

How immature I
Used to be. These days if I
Were to fall from a
Tree I'd splatter seeds and juice
All over the countryside.

I've never had so
Many people wishing me
A Happy Easter—
Buddhists, Jews, Muslims, Sikhs and
The occasional Christian.

Nobody's crying.
It's just the sound of my boots
    In the melting snow.

Ray's blood-soaked body—
Found on the path through the woods
    Halfway between his
Little cabin and the road
He was trying to crawl to.

She had a flair for
The exotic. We used to
    Arrange to meet in
London, Ont., or Paris, Ont.—
Even once in Rome, N.Y.

The sky's paved with stars.
What eyes the wise must have to
    See one vast mirror.

      "Oh, you don't have to
Pay me, I'll do it for free!"
      He had asked her if
She would like to become his
Executive assistant.

      Spring at Yonge and Bloor—
Some seem perfectly happy
      In T-shirts and shorts.
Others are shivering in
Parkas with their hoods pulled up.

      I dreamt my little
Life was the subject of a
      TV movie viewed
By millions on a planet
A thousand light years from here.

She had cartoon eyes.
I could never remember
Which of them was blind.

Spent the afternoon
Walking through the rain, looking
For my fountain pen.

When things aren't going
Well, give me a call. I have
An Estonian
Fairy tale about Good Luck.
It just might change things around.

Got my fingernail
Caught in my zipper. Had to
Get the library
Staff to help me get it free.
They said this happens often.

Notice guy reading
William Deverell's *Needles*.
    The same book. We smile.
"What page are you on?" "Forty-
Seven." "So am I." "How strange."

    Her teeth were even.
She smiled to excess but she
    Chewed with distinction.

    It's clear the Scotti
Were the same people as the
    Hiberni. So why
Do so many people ask
If you're Irish or Scottish?

    Oh, great mind of the
Universe, fill my little
    Mind with your sweet milk.

At the moment of
Mother's death my bed strangely
Collapsed under me.

I have good sense of
What is right and wrong for me
But no idea
Of what is right or wrong for
Other people and their kids.

Normally no one
Talks in the elevators
But if you comment
Upon it soon everyone
Is talking away like mad.

You stopped by my door
To chat a while and I prayed
For a sudden storm.

Stupid motorists
Driving to the store for a
      Pack of cigarettes—
So many that the streetcars
And buses get all tied up.

      With her expensive
Jewellery she was jealous
      Of him when he'd sit
And watch the way the sunlight
Sparkled in each drop of rain.

      "How can I stop my
Thoughts from racing?" She pointed
      At the sky. His eyes
Went up. "It's a beautiful
Sky," he said and then he died.

No better way to
Amuse oneself while strolling
　　Along Yonge Street than
Imagining one of those
Old World War II air attacks.

When I was sixteen
George Meyers said my hips were
　　Shaped like a woman's.
I almost died. Now I wish
I'd bought a dress and makeup.

Reading *Kokoro*
In the noodle joint. Waitress
　　Notices and smiles.
Says she found it too slow but
It's her mother's favourite book.

Sad about his death—
Travel to the funeral—
        Soon we're all laughing.

        I'm going to die
So when I write a poem
        I keep it simple.

        She used to think it
So poetic when I'd get
        Up at dawn and leave.

        Would you like me to
Bite off your earlobe? Then you
        Could tell everyone,
"Oh that? Why that was done by
The famous poet Genmai."

That scandalous dress
You wore last summer, your heart
Was as transparent.

She is looking out
At the undisturbed snow that's
Fallen overnight.
A visitor says to her,
"Where should I throw the tea leaves?"

The word on Genmai—
He's not ambitious enough.
Is that a bad thing?

She was seventeen
When I last saw her. Now she's
Fifty-five. It's true
She has changed in certain ways
But she still wears bobby socks.

You were lovely, I
Was tongue-tied, you said focus
On this, and this, and—

She said she'd be true
As long as her chemise stayed
Under my pillow.

She considered the
Lilies of the field. Now the
Whole town's scandalized.

Those scandalized by
Our behaviour are doomed to
Snore their lives away.

She found the flower
Of forgetting blooming in
    The cave of my heart.

You took me sailing
On the ship of love. Now I'm
    Shivering and sick.

Feeling awful but
I've felt awful before this—
    No doubt will again.

No one can blame me
For dreaming we are lying
    In each other's arms.

Summer nights are short!
Our eyes meet and already
The sun is rising!

She wants to go home
To see if anyone has
Sent her a haiku.

I'm terrified. I'm
Lying in bed with eyes closed.
When I open them
Will I find myself thirty
Years old or thirteen or three?

Sometimes I forget
How despicable I've been.
So you are welcome
To remind me whenever
You feel I need reminding.

That day when you were
Displeased with me the thing that
Hurt the most was this—
"Why do you always pretend
To be better than you are?"

I'm embarrassed and
Never learned to distinguish
Birds by their call. Or
By their feathers and their shape.
But I really like their beak.

Game? It was never
Meant to be a game—never!
This is baseball, pal!

Ideally, art's
A science. I don't study.
And look how it shows!

His phone number was
981-1036.
Dead at thirty-six.

"Roshi, why do you
Not emphasize satori?"
Before he answers
His wife says, "Because he has
Never experienced it!"

In a shower you
Know you're going to get wet.
But in a fog you
Don't know you're getting wet. You
Get wet little by little.

Canada is no
Place for perfect lines about
Frogs singing in ponds.

(after Michael Ondaatje)

Frogs sing in ponds soon
To be covered with houses—
   TV in each room.

   (after Daphne Marlatt's Steveston)

Who cares if nights are
Sleepless? I lie awake with
   Sonnets in my brain.

   (after bpNichol's Martyrology Book IV)

Science is boring.
I'd rather live in a fog
   Than know what caused it.

I love to touch the
Large warm blue light at each end
   Of station platforms.
From one end to the other
I walk, waiting for the train.

Age of miracles
Is over. I know. I tried
Walking on water.

When people say "I"
We feel ourselves being dragged
Down into smallness.

Her face and hands were
Three pure white flames but all the
Rest of her was black.

I'm my own best friend.
If I dislike a movie
I get up and leave—
No need to argue, not even
If I stay out all night long!

Sunday afternoon
As I read you sweet and
Tender passages
From *Breakfast at Tiffany's*
You give me a pedicure.

Woke up last night with
Someone squeezing my hand. It
Was my other hand.

Even holding hands
Is an ambiguous act,
More sour than sweet. It's
An act of desperation,
A political statement.

We know the entire
Universe is nothing but
A mirage, but still...

Compassion starts with
A spark and in a few days
       You're consumed with it.
Sometimes it comes late. When I
Look back I feel like dying.

       Ian sees I am
Torturing myself again.
       I tell him if I
Don't torture myself who will?
He says give nature a chance.

       Young ladies looking
For lovers weave necklaces
       Of summer flowers.
            (after Sappho)

       Such whiteness—the gulls
Under a black sky in the
       Early afternoon.

Summer's over and
Victor looks up to see his
Initial fly south.

Far from home, timid
Timas sends a purple scarf.
In my dream I see
The same scarf being worn by
A smiling Aphrodite.

(after Sappho)

Two eggs from the same
Chicken drop to the same floor.
One breaks, one doesn't.

Mom and Dad, you weren't
My real mom and dad but you
Couldn't have known that.

Whether or not we're
Sports-minded we all perhaps
Have our own secret
Batting averages, win-loss
Records and sense of the crowd.

Sixteen peaches sit
In a row on the branch of
My window. They do
Penance for being too hard.
Hurry on and soften up!

That busboy knows his
Beeswax, at first I thought he
Owned the bloody joint—
Next thing I know he's doing
Back flips up and down the bar.

I am a king who
Has three daughters, a daughter
Who has two sisters.

Look coldly at the
Cherry blossoms, they are chains
Binding us to pain.
(after Izumi Shikibu)

Where are you, Judy?
Have you run away with your
Haiku translator?
Or have you just taken a
Terrible dislike to me?

Tanka is to me
As bicycles to Curnoe.
His friends kept thinking
This was the end of the line
But it was merely the start.

How the hell did you
Manage to fall off a horse
That was standing still?
(after Robert Kroetsch)

I dreamed I was a
Simpleton looked after by
My loving sister.
(after Stuart MacKinnon)

The kids float sticks down
The creek behind the campsite
While we sip coffee.
(after Don McKay)

Out of the ashes,
Awakened by my burning
Cigarette—a moth.
(after Robin Blaser)

I keep trying to
Bite my pencil with a tooth
Gone five years ago.
(after George Bowering)

I ignore the real
Pigeon shit splattered on the
Bronze Napoleon.
(after Roy Kiyooka)

She says she doesn't
Mind but she says it as if
She minds a whole lot.

Painful to look at—
A freshly dug grave and a
Freshly written poem.

In the morning wind
A hundred ping-pong balls come
    Bouncing on Phipps Street.

    Rainy-day haiku—
But nothing is getting wet.
    The sun has turned green.

    People drive by with
Not a thought of what's going
    On in the bushes.

    On the dark street a
Slow grey moth fluttered around
    A self-illumined
Barber pole like a living
Neoplatonist.

Strange that fish don't sleep.
Must be all those coffee grounds
Going down the sink.

My dog has been out
All day in this rainstorm and
He's dry as a bone.

We got on the plane
And flew around the planet
Eyes open for plants.

Why do we worry?
We're merely leaves on a tree.
Let the tree worry.

Haiku from Auden

Arms around each other's necks,
    Inert, vaguely sad.

We must lose our loves—
On each beast and bird that moves
    Turn an envious look.

One has often seen
Shoes, but who saw a cardboard
    Lotus bud before?

Red slippers in a
Window; and in the street, flaws
    Of grey, windy sleet!

And now Yeats seeks in
His books and manuscripts what
He shall never find.

What made that sound? A
Rat, water-hen or otter
Slid into the stream.

All dreams of the soul
End in a beautiful man's
Or woman's body.

The soul's loneliness
Shudders in many cradles;
Memory is changed.

Because you've never
Jumped and laughed your thought is weak—
Clear, half out of life.

Someone has put out
The light in the high tower.
Bats rise from the trees.

With trees in blossom
All along the Niagara Gorge
We talk of Bali!

My dwelling is small—
I wouldn't need it at all
Except for the rain.

(after Zen priest Buccho, Basho's teacher)

It was a dull day.
He was weeping, and the leaves
        Were falling like tears.
They fell slowly in the rain,
Like a heavy, slower rain.

        There's a name for those
Who decide to burn all their
        Haikus and then don't.

        All my books are in
Boxes. It's almost time for
        Me to be erased.

        Big mind reclines in
The shade and eats bananas.
        Little mind paces
The floor and dreams up new ways
Of making life miserable.

The snow's gone but still
Mount Tsukuba shines as sweet
In its violet robes.

(after Basho)

No one can pass by
Mount Tsukuba and not write
A poem of his own.

(after Basho)

We sat in silence
Watching the cloudy moonlight,
Listening to the rain.

(after Basho)

We went into a
Fisherman's hut and had a
Short and smelly sleep.

(after Basho)

"Bury, oh bury
Your strange secret in my breast!"
The girl's heart cried out.

(from A Glastonbury Romance*)*

The deer are calling
For their mates. It's unlikely
I'll sleep deep tonight.

(after Ono No Komachi)

I can't finish my
Weaving, Mother. It's all sweet
Aphrodite's fault.
She's come close to killing me
With love for that cross-eyed boy.

(after Sappho)

Such a storm! The wind
Picks up the leaves and puts them
Back onto the trees.

Sitting in the tub
Eating a big orange on a
     Cool August morning—
Everyone has the best seat
In the house, declares John Cage.

Since I met you I've
Been happy all the time. But
     I was before too.

We are the greatest
Country in the world I'd say.
     Which is saying knots.

Dance is the only
Word that starts with D on a
     Day like yesterday.

O'Hara hated
"Subject matter"—and thirty
Years after his death
People including me are
Still writing poems about him.

Excellent student—
A pleasure to have in my
Class and now she's dead!

Five good things about
The countryside. People have
Time to shoot the shit!

Giant Easter egg
Found on Easter Island one
Easter long ago.

Hand me an H for
Every time good old Barrie
Pops into my mind.

Of course I love you
But you are on the ship and
I am on the shore.
(after "Harbour Lights" by
Hugh Williams & Jimmy Kennedy)

Inland from the coast
About a mile please bury
Me among the trees.

Jump up and down on
The earth with bare feet for long
Enough and you'll die.

Krazy Kat, I don't
Want to go to heaven if
You'll be somewhere else.

My golly, am I
Still alive? It's been years and
Years. How have I been?

Hamilton was my
Place of birth. But now I want
To die in Port Hope.

Two nice things about
Toronto. The sunsets, the
Moon and a sailboat.

Winter's on its way.
You've got a point there, my friend.
Hope for a long one.

Think it's easy to
Be a poet? We have to
Play the cards we're dealt.

I sit in the dark.
You appear in a huge egg
Of light and smiling.

It's been three weeks since
You died. If you think you've missed
Anything, you're nuts.

Warmongers! You don't
Know what it's like to die, or
        See your daughter die.

Why am I climbing
Imaginary mountains?
        Because they're not there.

A bunch of buddhas
Play bridge on a plane flying
        In and out of clouds.

In Victoria
The cherries are blossoming.
        I walk for a while
Then go to the library
And read Issa and Basho.

One man burns designs
With a magnifying glass
   In his alpenstock.
One man plays the saxophone.
Afternoon at the harbour!

My heart is shaggy,
Nervous, loyal, and its tongue
   Slobbers like a dog's.

After my reading
Nineteen-year-old Rebecca
   Presented me with
A brown silk smoking jacket—
Sprayed with sixteen subtle scents.

Why am I writing
Imaginary haiku?
   Because they're not there.

The light when you snuff
A candle, where does it go?
        Or does it just die?

        If I could see my
Self as others see me I'd
        Be lost without you.

        I don't look for it
And it doesn't look for me.
        I gave up despair.

        Rude of you last night—
Singing "Bye Bye Baby" in
        Marilyn Monroe's voice
Non-stop on the telephone
While my new friend was waiting.

Bulldozers tear down
Small trees while small fledglings gorge
Themselves on cut worms.

(after Frank Davey)

Everybody was
Going with the flow except
For me and my dog.

Bissett reads the news:
"Salmon talks continuing.
Glug glug glug glug glug."

Kid bites his finger.
Doesn't he get meat at home?
I had a bump on
My head the size of my head—
Now it's shrunk to nothing, kid.

Why does that tramp have
Lilac blotches on his cheeks?
Only the storks know.

(After Nikolai Gumilyov's The Plague*)*

Happy birthday, Self.
Your life has been one mistake
After another.

Serenity in
A plane going down in flames.
That's the holy grail.

No one, Norris, likes
Unsolicited advice.
But please remember—
Make sure you've planted the vines
Before you start planting trees.

(after Horace's "Book I Ode XVIII")

She says my poems
Are not terribly Zen-like.
Shall I try harder?

Why should we worry?
We're just water in the tub.
Let the tub worry.

Dragonfly clings to
The underside of a leaf
Battered by the storm.

(after Velemir Khlebnikov)

The lake lies back and
Like a weary old woman
Looks into the sky.
She cares for little, she just
Reflects sunrise and sunset.

(after Aleksander Blok)

Excuse me, dear, I'm
Trying to write a haiku.
What season is this?

On Government Street
Some con men try to sell me
Hare Krishna books.
"I'm already enlightened,"
I say. So they ask for cash.

Life's one big free lunch,
Even in times of famine.
Death is the dessert.

Wandering among
Blossoming trees everyone's
A complete stranger.

Go ahead! Shoot me—
I won't stop kissing the hoof
Of this weary old horse.

(after Khlebnikov's "War in a Mousetrap")

She was lovelier
To look upon than pear trees
In profuse blossom.

(after Chaucer's "Miller's Tale")

The universe sings.
Tibetan Buddhists sing. The
Universe sings twice.

I phone my father
And tell him the cherry trees
Bloom all year long here
In Victoria, B.C.
He seems to believe me too!

Down Niagara Gorge
A cherry tree in blossom—
Who'd have noticed it?

Someday you'll see me
In a bus full of old folks
Touring through scenic
Lilacs, blossoming fruit trees.
Remember! Blow me kisses!

Thousands of runners,
Yonge Street, Sunday morning, none
Having any fun.

Dogen Dogen the
Dogen Dogen thought of no
Dogen Dogen thought.

One selfish thought, the
Universe loses all its
    Vast empty spaces.

I am seventy—
The wound I've been suffering
    Since birth is healing.

At a time like this
Who can think of poetry?
    Nobody, that's who.

I thought up a good
Title for a spy novel:
    Aspiring Spy Ring.
I will never write it though.
You can have it if you want.

Telephones make me
Sad when they don't ring, scared to
Answer when they do.

She thinks I'm a twerp
Since I've started using my
Middle initial.

I'd give anyone
Ten to one we sure won't get
Out of here alive.

I hereby renounce
Newspapers, radio, and
TV. By sitting
Zazen for two hours a day
I'll make my contribution.

My mother has died
And I never told her how
Beautiful she was.

The last hummingbird
Is at my window but I'm
Zazen zazen zaz...

Unsheltered in his
Naked nudity, he felt
Sad and sorrowful.

(after Flann O'Brien)

Last week while touring
The west coast five and seven
Syllable lines filled
My mind. In Toronto I
Find I have to work for it.

A driver kindly
Stopped to let us cross the street—
        Ian, Annie, Skye,
Hailey, Sheena and Genmai.
He resembled Greg Curnoe.

Now that I'm older
I don't get angry often.
        When I do I get
Angry with myself or when
I don't I feel enlightened.

Constantly John writes
Novel after novel. His
        First got bad reviews.
He no longer even tries
To get published anymore.

Annie and Ian
Read Takuboku poems
        At that wedding feast.
The groom died ten years ago
Age forty of lung cancer.

        To me these lines of
Five and seven syllables
        Sound like the booming
And beating of giant drums
In tenth-century Japan.

        People ask me why
I added a W
        To my name. I say
No one would ever crown me
So I had to crown myself.

Waiting for a bus
I ask an older lady
        For change for a two.
Just then a cab stops and I
Hop in. She gives me a look.

We dream of sailing
Through the islands with a friend.
        Awaken at four—
I go walking through the night
With Henry James in pocket.

When I look down to
When I was twenty it seems
        Like a small hop. But
When I got to be fifty
Seemed an impossible climb.

Ian McConnell
Says, "Life is showbiz." If you
        Disagree he smiles
And says, "Who made you the hall
Monitor anyway, pal?"

In Victoria
Everywhere you look you see
        Blossoming cherries,
Blue mountains in the distance—
A stepping stone to heaven.

In Seattle the
Ducks doze on docks and silent
        Seaplanes float by. Just
Flew in from Victoria
And thinking of flying back.

Back in Toronto
My place is cold and messy.
Flying all night long
Then sleeping all day till five
Now my mind is full of thoughts.

Skye and Hailey came
To my poetry reading.
They said most poems
Aren't real but mine truly are—
Especially the tanka.

Annie and Ian
Didn't come to my reading.
They said they preferred
Knowing me as a human being
Than as a famous poet.

Fort Street afternoon—
All the people so nicely
Dressed, on the verge of
Smiling, and possessed of the
Secrets of the catacombs.

Imagine! Fifty-
Five and still my poetry's
Unknown in other
Lands, and in Canada it's
Ridiculed and vilified.

Michelangelo's
Version of the Spark goes from
God's finger into
Man's. Why not heart to heart or
Mind to mind? Arm's-length funding?

Sorry, no TV
Or even radio. Her
Only phobias.
There are people out there she
Can't see but can see/hear her.

"If you don't get back
In your cab you'll be sorry."
He gets back in and
Drives off. I'm very relieved—
He was going to kill me!

Last night I watched a
Film Jack Lemmon made when he
Was my age. Today
Someone strangely remarked that
I look just like Jack Lemmon.

My stool takes the shape
Of a perfect letter S
        (Sans serif). Nature
Reminds me I'm supposed to
Return to Scotland this year.

        Give me those who aren't
Afraid to say "I don't know."
        You can have the rest.

        The Wings of the Dove
Suddenly seems to be by
        John B. Boyle. All the
People in his paintings are
Characters in the novel.

        You're a rock. Punch you
In the nose they'll break their hands.
        All they can do is
Chip away at you till you're
Nothing but the air you breathe.

Amy Singer, she's
A diabetic, age five.
    She carries around
Her own little bag of sweets.
Now and then she takes a sniff.

    My wife used to say,
"You're a loner. You should be
    Living by yourself
Or with someone just like you."
I was shocked but she was right.

    Oh great mind of the
Universe, fill my little
    Bottle with your milk.

    If God is love and
Love is blind how can God see
    Little sparrows fall?

A woman's standing
On a hill and shaking her
    Fist at the flying
Saucers in the sky above—
"Come and get me, you bastards!"

When some ill-bred chap
Insults you today it helps
    You forget the rude
And nasty comments other
People have made in the past.

Don't put your hand in
Your pocket abruptly when
    Strangers are around.

Oh, I get it now!
Haiku is to tanka as
    Morning mist to swamp.

I liked it better
When in perfect innocence
   One could tell a girl
She was beautiful without
A lengthy analysis.

   Ah, vanity! I
So loved that poem I wanted
   To write the author—
But then realized that it
Had been written by *moi-même*.

   At the reception
When he'd read his poems I
   Went up to him and
Introduced myself. He looked
Horrified and walked away.

"Alison, look. There's
A street named after you!" She
        Beams with pleasure. In
The back seat her sister bursts
Into tears and sobs and sobs.

        Tiny volcano
All covered with snow sits on
        The curved horizon
Of the red planet Mars—a
Picture of my glaucoma.

        Before leaping out
Of bed this morning I read
        Three stories—by E.
Pauline Johnson, Mazo de
La Roche, Adeline Teskey.

Was that your father
Who used woodpecker scalps for
The ashes of his
Fragrant *dimanches eternels*
Or was it some other dad?

Prokofiev was
Ill and couldn't attend the
Performance of his
Piano sonata. He
Listened to it on the phone.

When he died the sky
Was blue. Then the clouds came and
It started to rain.
At that moment I lost my
Lovely gold pen on Yonge Street.

Hi! We're having a
Get-together in this poem
    Friday night at eight.

If he is ever
Found murdered the suspect list
    Would be a mile long.
He makes me helpless with hate
And I'm not the only one.

My horses are wild
With spring, they long for distant
    Fields where light mists rise.

My only chance to
See you now is in my dreams—
    But I'm wide awake!

All night the sound of
Pouring rain mingles with the
Chanting of the monks.

The extreme hatred
I felt for that poor fellow
Who's doing his best—
It merely turned out to be
Disguised hatred for myself.

Come quickly! I have
In my hand a flower that
Blossoms and then fades.

In the warm dark night
I awaken to the scent
Of a plum blossom.

(after Izumi Shikibu)

Compared with love, the
Cherry blossoms and snowdrops
Are here forever.

A warm wind scatters
The cherry blossoms, and my
Heart feels a deep chill.

She's loose and adrift.
Any stream inviting her
To come she'd follow.

Mix up your proverbs
All you can thanks to Victor
Who once told me that
The grass is always greener
At the end of the tunnel.

    I would follow you
Like a ripple follows the
        Breeze on Demon Pond.

        Even in my dreams
I find I have to pretend
        That I don't know you.

        My morning glories
Are hiding this morning. What
        Are they ashamed of?

        Throw yourself in front
Of a train, what a waste! But
        If you get a cop
To shoot you you'll become a
Martyr and a *cause célèbre*.

You appear and if
I knew I was dreaming I'd
        Keep sleeping all night.

        Bought a book on Zen
In a little Buddhist store.
        Gave owner the old
Line about "buying water
By the river." He said, "What?"

        You don't feel well. You
Lie down and think about death.
        Soon you feel better.

        "Awoke this morning
Eager and willing to do
        A day's work"—This is
What my grandfather wrote in
His diary every day.

If it can't be said
In seventeen syllables
Why bother with it?

If it can't be said
In seventeen syllables
Or thirty-one, it...

This is the best book
I've ever read, I don't want
To miss a word. I
Want to read through to the end
Then I can die happily.

People who hear the
Sound of the pine trees on a
Windy day write poems—
But it's really just the pines
Standing in the blowing wind.

It's been a long time
Since my last anonymous
      Cheque came in the mail.

      I'm standing on a
Platform waiting for a train—
      Nothing more to say.

      Editing error—
In *Angels and Insects* the
      Card-playing scene should
Have come before he finds his
Wife in bed with her brother.

      There was a certain
Fundamental thing about
      Zen I didn't know.
Now that's all cleared up I can
Live my life with no problems.

Gathering info
From various sources, you'll
End up ignorant—
But if your mind is clear, true
Knowledge is already yours.

When our mind's empty
It's like a dark sky. Lightning
Flashes and the sky's
Dark again. When the mind's dark
We prepare for the lightning.

She always wants to
Make love in abandoned old
Greasy garages
Over by the steel mills of
Hamilton, Ontario.

E-mail's okay but
The Internet is boring.
Better to sit still
All night holding your mother's
Hand as she prepares to die.

The richer you get
The richer you want to be—
The older you get
The older you want to be.
It should be the opposite.

The poorer I get
The poorer I want to be—
The younger I get
The younger I want to be.
Used to be the opposite.

It's been great having
Tom Wayman around this year.
Every line of his
Poetry always has the
Right number of syllables!

Tom Wayman and I
Have different philosophies
But always manage
To get along famously—
Because we have no ego!

Andrew's kid sister—
Until last night she never
Met a poet or
Attended a reading. Now
She's a huge Stuart Ross fan.

Anne Frank wanted to
Be famous—to give pleasure
Even to people
She'd never meet and even
After her life was over.

The poems we write
After the Holocaust must
Be the type Hitler
Would have despised, that would have
Had us put in cattle cars.

Anne Frank heard on the
BBC that diaries
Would be much valued
When the war was over—so
She rewrote hers from the top!

The camp guard in an
Overcoat up to his eyes
        To the prisoner
Standing naked in the snow—
"They will never believe this!"

    A voice said to me—
When you die you're off to a
        Planet just like this
But lighter than air and pure.
So start cleaning up your act.

        Dad laughs at old guy
Wearing belt and suspenders.
        "He's hedging his bets."
Thirty years later Dad starts
Wearing belt and suspenders!

In my dream painting
Was competitive like chess.
I put down a stroke
Then opponent did the same.
Picasso was hard to beat.

Big mind floats like a
Popsicle stick. Little mind
Worries about the
State of his wardrobe and if
His poems will bring him fame.

Big mind floats to the
Top and spreads its arms and legs.
Little mind divebombs
Straight to the bottom and spends
Its life dreaming of revenge.

Big mind offers an
Open hand while little mind
Offers a closed fist.

Should I stay or go?
That is the question that has
Bugged me all my life.
As soon as I have answered
Once I have to ask again.

Neo-cons are big
Liars. Their biggest whopper—
"There is no free lunch."

Ah, literature,
There's nothing about it I
Don't know. —Nabokov

Who composes to
His own liking takes a hard
        Parting from men's love.

        Love is what you feel
For everyone you meet, while
        Infatuation
Is what you feel for someone
You want to spend your life with.

        Big mind is the fog
That socks us in and the light
        Guiding us from grief.
Little mind doesn't notice
Any fog or light—just grief.

        In the woods for love—
We end up getting eaten
        By ferocious bears.

Such lovely things as
Postage stamps and lighthouses
Are disappearing
While on a huge growth curve are
Ugly things like cars and guns.

The Great Guru says
Being "fully realized"
Is such a bore. To
Descend to our level, he
Gets drunk and falls through windows.

Terrible typo
In Whitney Smith's business cards.
They came out "Shitney."
But he is so nonchalant
He hands them out anyway!

Practising my Welsh—
I stopped a fellow and asked
Inadvertently
If he could direct me to
The nearest decimal point.

I'm sobbing at the
Tomb of the Unknown Soldier.
Two Cockney con men
Spotted me and managed to
Relieve me of fifty quid.

The lips of my heart
Whisper to me that my verse
Will live forever.
If the jealous disagree
I'm hardly bothered at all.

Through the years my friends
Must have known that I'm not real.
Why do they persist
In pretending that I'm real?
Maybe it's that they're not real!

Until now I thought
Everyone was real but me.
In a flash that's changed
And now I see it was just
My way of being special.

Free love or free verse—
When would you like it? But free
Sushi—no such thing.

Nice things happen to
Nice people on lovely nights
In or out of bed.

He'll piss on a book
If he doesn't like it. If
He feels trapped at some
Dull party he'll go to the
Bathroom and piss on the floor.

I'm a subjective
Man. I never ask questions.
I just work it out.

That jerk who wrote *The
Green Hotel*, there's a photo
Of him stashed away
In her jewellery box and
I'm a little bit jealous!

The world is full of
Enlightened people who have
Never heard of Zen.

As I search for my
Fountain pen my father calls
        And says our old friend
Doug Morrell has died. My pen
Shows up in an old jacket.

        Sixty years later
Sandra Brody's mother says,
        There is no one who
Remembers the blue dress I
Wore in nineteen thirty-three.

        When you're ninety, says
Grandma, people you haven't
        Seen in fifty years
Appear so real in your dreams
You can reach out and touch them.

Hungry at midnight—
Two pints of Guinness and two
       Packages of crisps
At the old Jack Russell Pub
Across the street from my place.

       Merlin and I, lost
Late at night in Forest Hill,
       Shining with thick rain,
Stop to check the unfolding
Tender leaves of well-kept trees.

       Sincere people don't
Smile as easily as I.
       What shall I do? Learn
To smile less? Be more sincere?
Quit looking in the mirror?

Often my tongue and
Heart are at cross-purposes.
I didn't mean to
Badmouth language poetry.
Better than no poetry!

Tina Beauregard—
Practitioners bright and dull
In every school. I'm
Receptive and ready to
Enfold all things to my heart.

Form is the signal
That the content is worthy
To be cared about.

Everyone is their
Own artist and the world is
One big Art Machine.

They're tearing down my
School. Soon it will be no more.
Trying not to cry.
People die as is well-known.
Schools need to be torn down.

If I wanted to
Have a "thing" I'd paint my nose
Black every morning
And dye my hair sky-blue but
Then my cover would be blown.

Fourteen times I've seen
Spring blossoming here and there
Around Toronto—
One time for every line in
"Shall I compare thee to a—"

Blond blue-eyed kid to
Mama when she says he can
      Have anything he
Wants for lunch. But will they have
Anything I want? Silence.

      In the theatre
Lady on my right has a
      Load of firewood
On her lap, and little logs
Keep rolling onto my lap.

      I'm fifty and all
My old friends have died or switched
      To writing fiction.
But I'm still writing poems,
Trapped in high school forever.

New York consciousness?
That fight has been fought, my friend.
        Regionalism—
Its drumbeats can be heard in
Every village on the globe.

        "International
Awareness" used to mean we
        Were naive to think
Anything from anywhere
Was as good as from New York.

        When I was a kid
Everyone with Irish, French
        Or Italian names
Used to go to Mass each week.
Now it's not like that. Things change.

Hi, honey, I'm home!
Big Boy's beat. Where did all these
Bloody bees come from?

As a child, I used
To run the slide projector
At Sunday school. Our
Missionaries among the
Haida. So much work to do.

Roaring motorbikes
With no mufflers bother me
Not at all. It's my
Nutty aunts Edith and Joyce
Arriving out of nowhere.

Swat! Swat! Swat! Swat! Swat!
Swat! Swat! Swat! Swat! Swat! Swat! Swat!
Dozen undone flies!

When I was a kid
I could walk so quietly
     Through the woods that once
Without any warning I
Saw a dozen dozing deer.

     Crad was upset. They
Wouldn't run his ad: Retired
     Axe Murderer Seeks Mate—
"How can someone live without
Having a sense of humour."

     Man is the membrane
That divides heaven from hell—
     The skin of the big
Bass drum at the head of the
Scottish bagpipe marching band.

What a jerk I've been—
All those hours I've wasted in
    Wrestling with my will.
Never again will I sit
In Buddhist meditation.

    I lose everything!
Only thing I don't lose is
    My poetry book.

    Do you ever feel
That you've been sitting in a
    Warm bath all your life?

    Just point at yourself
And say, "Zen Buddhist." Beggars
    Will leave you alone.

Day by day I pile
Bills and poems on my desk
By the computer.
One day I'll decide which of
Each I'll save or throw away.

The canvas on which
Everything is painted is
Apologetic.
I just happened to catch my
Eye on a corner of it.

Its duty is to
Make sure no one knows it's there—
Behind the grey clouds,
Behind the tall buildings like
Something solid in a sea.

Though my eye is black
It doesn't hurt at all. It's
      As if it's someone
Else's. So now I know it's
There. End of speculation.

      As he lay dying
He called his killer "crazy."
      Replied the killer—
"I'm not crazy, you're the one
Going to the hospital."

      Playing as a child
In Gage Park I never knew
      That poets such as
Al Purdy and others too
Would one day read poems there.

This is not a knot—
But it's true there's something of
   A not in a knot.
In the middle of my mind
Is a lovely sailor's knot.

   For forty years now
I've thought and thought about Zen.
   What an idiot!

   Who was that fellow
Who each day for twenty years
   Would clap his hands, dance,
Laugh and sing: "Bodhisattvas,
Come right now and get your rice"?

   I forget who taught
Me to pull my nose hairs out
   So it wouldn't hurt.

Lady in the park
Calls her dog "Humanity."
      I think she's my style.

If someday you see
Me in a bus full of old-
      Timers touring through
Lilac-and-cherry-blossom
Scenery blow me a kiss.

Most beautiful word
(In English) (if you ask me)
      Is "forget-me-not."

Love to feel your warm
Breath in the crook of my arm.
      Either arm will do.

So much beauty in
My life at last. I'd be sad
        If I died. There are
Many like me for sure but
You're the only one for me.

        All we know is what's
In our mind but then again
        What's not in our mind?
It encircles us like a
Transparent blue horizon.

        At Niagara Falls
I was only a few feet
        From going over.
Now I'm back in Toronto
As if it never happened.

Hanging around with
Genmai is just like living
Inside a poem.
Unfortunately, of course,
It'd be a Genmai poem.

A monument to
Sweet respectability—
Niagara-on-the-
Lake, where, I predict, G. B.
Shaw will someday be reborn.

When he heard my name
He asked if I wrote poems and
If I'd been in the
Same school as Barrie Nichol.
I said no, we were just friends.

I think I told him
I write too much. He said I
Shouldn't write at all.

Eating something here—
Disgusting but delicious.
Reading something here—
D. T. Suzuki's *Role of*
Nature in Zen Buddhism.

To the waitress at
Fran's—"How exactly do you
Squeeze your oranges?"

Sweet girl in the tube
Looked like Charlotte Gainsborough.
I shyly eyed her
As she counted her money—
Seven twenties and a ten.

Charlotte Gainsborough
Saw me eyeing her and took
From her pocket a
Chocolate bar and sullenly
And poutingly devoured it.

Man wearing a "Go
To Heaven" T-shirt is a-
Sleep on the subway.

Leaving for Scotland—
I saw a dead mouse with a
Snake coiled around it.

Upon arrival
In a new city I'd take
The bus to the zoo
And all around town. Don't know
Why I don't do that these days.

I don't want to go
Suddenly like Greg Curnoe.
I want to go slow.

U.S. tourist in
Glasgow Airport: "This is still
The British Empire!"

After flying to
Cuba with Canadians
I'll never complain
Again as long as I live
About the Americans.

Twilight evening dusk
Close of day nightfall sundown
Sunset eventide.

There should be a zoo
Especially for animals
    Like Jon, me and you.

Ancestral alert—
The smell of burning peat and
    The taste of Laphroaig.

It's hard to forget
The miseries of childhood.
    Yet our minds drift off
And revisit childhood haunts
And all ugliness has gone.

George has just returned
From Victoria where he
    Saw twenty-one plays
By Samuel Beckett. Now he'll
Have lunch with Willy at Art's.

Those who live longer
Will get the biggest applause
When they reach heaven.

Notoriety
Is bad luck. My books are all
You would want to know.

Frozen with self-doubt—
I work around the clock then
Go away for months.

Odd how you forgot
My phone number and address
Twice in the past year.
Or have you just got tired of
Me reciting poems to you?

My brother says that
Everyone is stupid. They
      Leave their cars running.

In a house far from
The road, we sit up all night
      With our minds afire.

      I gave the guy hell
Because his apples were stale—
      What's come over me?
Banging my head with my fist—
Should I start smoking hashish?

      I wrote on the wall,
"You are going to die soon."
      Next day somebody
Erased what I had written
And scribbled "Victoria!"

Thirty years ago
Victor Coleman asked me—Was
        Blake superstitious?
Last night I told him I still
Haven't quite made up my mind.

        Jenny predicts I'll
Have a great time in Scotland.
        That's the thing about
Europe, she declares. They're so
Much more with it over there.

        Today I woke up
With a mad desire to write
        Poems of five lines.

        I seem fated to
Die slowly. Can't recall when
        I last fell in love.

The nineties are the
Sixties upside down. But what
Ever happened to
The seventies and eighties?
Oh my God, they're just a blur!

He told me I should
Write a lot less, I said he
Shouldn't write at all.

I'm a simple man—
Too dumb for the neighbourhood
Trivia team, too
Dumb to cheat at bowling, too
Dumb for notoriety.

Feathers on the dot.
Daughters on the feather. The
Broadview bus goes by.

She doesn't seem to
See it's dead, its skin and head
    Are stuffed with clay. She
Jumps on it and she finds the
Rabbit hanging from the tree.

    After their springtime
Rock around the clock the bulls
    Have no intentions.

    A vicious-looking
Sabre-toothed goat's chasing me
    Down suburban streets.
I yell at it to take off
But it keeps coming at me.

    Silence is the way.
Silence is the way to hell.
    Silence is the way.

I'll write a perfect
Poem then I'll fly away
      To poem heaven.

      Crying in the dark—
"Don't let it ruin your life"
      Your voice seems to say.

      Issa had Basho—
But I am such a scoundrel
      There's no one for me.

      Behind the mask of
Beauty ugliness, behind
      Ugliness beauty—
Childhood instincts grow into
Trusted adult axioms.

High-school wrestling team
Gets fired up when the coach bites
Heads off live sparrows.

Sometimes I see them
Hand in hand, and study them.
Then I look away.

Schoenberg's self-portraits—
Viewers said they wished they were
Blind as well as deaf.

You think of me as
David McFadden, I think
Of me as Genmai
Thinking of himself as Miles
Davis and/or Marcel Proust.

It's stopped raining but
Still my window is flecked with
        Raindrops big and small.

        All activity
Is alchemical. We are
        Always trying to
Deny that essentially
Everything is nothingness.

        Get your mind off it.
Be serene. She's not going
        To die now she can
Finally breathe after all
These years. That'd be too cruel.

        Among those clowns who
Wear red sponge balls on their nose
        High lung cancer rate!

The reader lives a
Thousand lives, the non-reader
Lives but one (or two).

I've never known an
Atheist claim believers
Are headed for hell.

Sometimes a photo
Is so good you want to take
A photo of it.

Life's a chemical
Soup in which the nicer you
Are the less you're liked.

Turns out the love in
Love songs is true. Everything
Will last forever.
The wind blows a gust of rain
All over my desk and me.

Clever of God to
Create numerable stars.
How did he do it?

In a previous
Life I had my own spaceship
And would go around
Checking out all the black holes
All around the universe.

She comes in colours
Everywhere. She combs her hair.
She's like a rainbow.

I'm on a tightrope
Walking across Niagara.
But then aren't we all?

All night under my
Window two widows making
Beautiful music.

He was a Maoist
In his seventies. But now
He expresses shock
When he finds out that I don't
Have cable television.

We're all polar bears
Adrift on melting ice floes
Wondering what next.
Watching the spider approach—
How is it different from me?

Born brokenhearted.
Only now are the pieces
Coming together.

Now that I'm sixty
I begin to awaken
From an ugly dream.

One day I woke up.
Noticed the thorn in my side.
Pulled it out myself.

A bird killed my fish.
So for years I hated birds.
What a waste of time.

I spent six decades
In a bubble. When it burst
Nothing really changed.

My place is a mess.
I just sit here reading books
And writing poems.

In my dreams I sit
Drinking wine and laughing with
All my former friends.

I spent sixty years
Trying to impress people.
What an idiot!

Dead people aren't dead.
They've become permanently
Unavailable.

There's only one way
Of being born. But there are
Many ways to die.

The past is dead, the
Future is dead, the present
Is on its last legs.

The sun burns, the earth
(Thank God for commas) rotates,
The heart beats and beats.

We try to see from
Every possible angle
Every chance we get.

So it is! You must
Have a high IQ. But what
About the bookshelves?

Sometimes we have to
Try hard to see that the past
Never existed.

My mother is so
Considerate that if my
Father died she would
Wait until the morning light
Before she gives me a call.

The cold and slimy
Water in the muddy ditch.
Big rat jumps in. Plop.

In the days of the
Ancient gods this big tree must
Have been a seedling.

Medium massage.
Winter has come and gone. Turn
Off your computer.

I'd never heard a
Veteran of armed combat
Speak so casually.

There's more to haiku
Than you realize. You smiled
Then said go on. Click.

In the falling leaves
A man is drinking whisky.
His dog is snoring.

A tiny insect
In a silent house makes a
Scary cracking sound.

That note you left me.
I've forgotten what it said.
Do you remember?

Boing boing boing boing boing
Boing boing (Spring Haiku) boing boing
Boing boing boing boing boing.

Nosferatu, that
Man you brought in today has
Gone out of his mind.

For fifty years now
I've been reading about Zen.
What an idiot!

Beautiful picture.
I'm very glad I met you.
We look terrific.

Every atom in
My body was forged in fire—
A faraway fire.

When spring arrives the
Flowers appear and it starts
To get Darth Vader.

By the time I have
This figured out it will have
Become obsolete.

There he is running
Past the Science Store on Yonge—
Observe a Tory!

I thought we were friends
Forever but now you've got
        More important friends.

        Boing boing boing boing boing
Boing boing (Gary Barwin) boing
        Boing boing boing boing boing.

        Sailing in a sea
Of tears which as we all know
        Sparkle prettily.

        Technology sails—
Iceberg culture's inevit-
        Able as icebergs.

No grass this year but
Plenty of cherry blossoms
    Lying on the walk.

We commit ourselves
To the transparent cloud that
    Surrounds me and you.

The brain's a gland, you
Have to open it up and
    Then you dust it off.

The ABCs of
Writing fake haiku. You've got
    A point there, my friend.

Hand me an H for
Every time Happy Harris
Hops into my mind.

Golly, am I still
Alive? It's been years and years.
How am I doing?

I only phone long
Distance once a year. Christmas
And of course Easter.

November's the month
When dead dogs float down rivers
Never to return.

A pigeon leaves its
Mate on the fifth-floor ledge, dives
Down to the alley,
Picks up a piece of popcorn
And brings it back up with him.

A white man with black
Cadillac seeks black woman
With white Cadillac.

Salmon-coloured skies
In the morning or evening—
Salmon for dinner!

It comes to this—it's
Dusk now and I'm not going
Anywhere tonight.

Fifty-year-old man
In grey suit to younger man
          In blue suit: "We need
Real leadership at this point,
Not just perceived leadership."

          The falling rain sounds
Lovely as the quiet street.
          The ear and the eye
Are as different as the moon
And the sun. I have to pee.

          My girl friend says I'm
A megalomaniac
          Because I can't face
The world without wearing my
Brand-new Boulet cowboy boots.

If I open my
Window, I have to turn on
        The fan, or else the
Exhaust from the chicken joint
Next door fills my studio.

        Vacuuming for the
First time in months and notice
        The vacuum cleaner
Has become dusty. Need a
Smaller one to keep it clean.

        A small white bird flew
Over your moonlit shoulder
        Last night very late.

        Halfway down the gorge
A cherry tree in fruit—the
        Crows have noticed it.

Hesperus, herdsman
Of the evening, herds cattle
        Back to the barnyard,
Children back to their mothers,
Traffic back to the suburbs.

(after Sappho)

When the lights go out
And all the candles are snuffed
        We regard the stars!

She's just arrived from
Bucharest and has never
        Heard of streets like this.

Bodhisattva Vow—
It becomes more meaningful
        All of a sudden.

Poets show the way.
The dead don't die. They look on
　　And help when they can.

　　I'm no Jesus but
I wash my friends' feet and they
　　Drive spikes through my hands.

　　It's getting to be
So very predictable.
　　You go to bed with
Eva Braun, and you wake up
With Marlene Dietrich.

　　Secrets of long life—
Always keep the ends of your
　　Laces the same length.

I've felt weak all week.
I live alone. This morning
        After sleeping well
I got up to brush my teeth
And my toothbrush was all wet!

One selfish thought, the
Universe loses all its
        Vast empty spaces.

I'm not desperate—
Life has not smiled on me but
        I'm not desperate.

Sometimes I think I've
Resurrected haiku for
        The world. What a nut!

David W. McFadden has been publishing poetry since the early 1960s. He is the author of about thirty books of poetry, fiction, and travel writing. *Why Are You So Sad? Selected Poems of David W. McFadden* (Insomniac Press) was shortlisted for the 2008 Griffin Prize for Poetry, and *Be Calm, Honey* (Mansfield Press) was shortlisted for the 2009 Governor General's Award for Poetry (his third such nomination). In 2013, *What's the Score?* (Mansfield Press) won the Griffin Prize for Poetry. David lives in Toronto.

OTHER BOOKS FROM MANSFIELD PRESS

Poetry

Leanne Averbach, *Fever*

Nelson Ball, *In This Thin Rain*

Gary Barwin, *Moon Baboon Canoe*

George Bowering, *Teeth: Poems 2006–2011*

Stephen Brockwell, *Complete Surprising Fragments of Improbable Books*

Stephen Brockwell & Stuart Ross, eds., *Rogue Stimulus: The Stephen Harper Holiday Anthology for a Prorogued Parliament*

Diana Fitzgerald Bryden, *Learning Russian*

Alice Burdick, *Flutter*

Alice Burdick, *Holler*

Jason Camlot, *What The World Said*

Margaret Christakos, *wipe.under.a.love*

Pino Coluccio, *First Comes Love*

Dani Couture, *YAW*

Gary Michael Dault, *The Milk of Birds*

Pier Giorgio Di Cicco, *The Dark Time of Angels*

Pier Giorgio Di Cicco, *Dead Men of the Fifties*

Pier Giorgio Di Cicco, *The Honeymoon Wilderness*

Pier Giorgio Di Cicco, *Living in Paradise*

Pier Giorgio Di Cicco, *Early Works*

Pier Giorgio Di Cicco, *The Visible World*

Salvatore Difalco, *What Happens at Canals*

Christopher Doda, *Aesthetics Lesson*

Christopher Doda, *Among Ruins*

Glenn Downie, *Monkey Soap*

Rishma Dunlop, *The Body of My Garden*

Rishma Dunlop, *Lover Through Departure: New and Selected Poems*

Rishma Dunlop, *Metropolis*

Rishma Dunlop & Priscila Uppal, eds., *Red Silk: An Anthology of South Asian Women Poets*

Ollivier Dyens, *The Profane Earth*

Jaime Forsythe, *Sympathy Loophole*

Carole Glasser Langille, *Late in a Slow Time*

Suzanne Hancock, *Another Name for Bridge*

Jason Heroux, *Emergency Hallelujah*

Jason Heroux, *Memoirs of an Alias*

Jason Heroux, *Natural Capital*

John B. Lee, *In the Terrible Weather of Guns*

Jeanette Lynes, *The Aging Cheerleader's Alphabet*

David W. McFadden, *Be Calm, Honey*

David W. McFadden, *What's the Score?*

Leigh Nash, *Goodbye, Ukulele*

Lillian Necakov, *The Bone Broker*

Lillian Necakov, *Hooligans*

Peter Norman, *At the Gates of the Theme Park*

Peter Norman, *Water Damage*

Natasha Nuhanovic, *Stray Dog Embassy*

Catherine Owen & Joe Rosenblatt, with Karen Moe, *Dog*

Corrado Paina, *The Alphabet of the Traveler*

Corrado Paina, *The Dowry of Education*

Corrado Paina, *Hoarse Legend*

Corrado Paina, *Souls in Plain Clothes*

Stuart Ross et al., *Our Days in Vaudeville*

Matt Santateresa, *A Beggar's Loom*

Matt Santateresa, *Icarus Redux*

Ann Shin, *The Last Thing Standing*

Jim Smith, *Back Off, Assassin! New and Selected Poems*

Jim Smith, *Happy Birthday, Nicanor Parra*

Robert Earl Stewart, *Campfire Radio Rhapsody*

Robert Earl Stewart, *Something Burned Along the Southern Border*

Carey Toane, *The Crystal Palace*

Priscila Uppal, *Summer Sport: Poems*

Priscila Uppal, *Winter Sport: Poems*

Steve Venright, *Floors of Enduring Beauty*

Brian Wickers, *Stations of the Lost*

Fiction

Marianne Apostolides, *The Lucky Child*

Sarah Dearing, *The Art of Sufficient Conclusions*

Denis De Klerck, ed., *Particle & Wave: A Mansfield Omnibus of Electro-Magnetic Fiction*

Paula Eisenstein, *Flip Turn*

Sara Heinonen, *Dear Leaves, I Miss You All*

Marko Sijan, *Mongrel*

Tom Walmsley, *Dog Eat Rat*

Non-Fiction

George Bowering, *How I Wrote Certain of My Books*

Rosanna Caira & Tony Aspler, *Buon Appetito Toronto*

Denis De Klerck & Corrado Paina, eds., *College Street–Little Italy: Toronto's Renaissance Strip*

Pier Giorgio Di Cicco, *Municipal Mind: Manifestos for the Creative City*

Amy Lavender Harris, *Imagining Toronto*

David W. McFadden, *Mother Died Last Summer*

For more information on these titles, and to order books, please visit www.mansfieldpress.net